General editor: Graham Handley

Brodie's Notes on Bill Naughton's

Spring and Port Wine

A. J. P. Smith BA

Pan Books London, Sydney and Auckland

First published 1988 by Pan Books Ltd,
Cavaye Place, London SW10 9PG
9 8 7 6 5 4 3 2 1
© Pan Books Ltd 1988
ISBN 0 330 50267 0
Photoset by Rowland Phototypesetting Ltd,
Bury St Edmunds, Suffolk
Printed and bound in Great Britain by
Richard Clay Ltd, Bungay, Suffolk

Contents

Page references are to the Samuel French edition of *Spring and Port Wine*, but the Notes may be used with any edition of the play.

Preface

The intention throughout this study aid is to stimulate and guide, to encourage the reader's *involvement* in the text, to develop disciplined critical responses and a sure understanding of the main details in the chosen text.

Brodie's Notes provide a summary of the plot of the play or novel followed by act, scene or chapter summaries each of which will have an accompanying critical commentary designed to underline the most important literary and factual details. Textual notes will be explanatory or critical (sometimes both), defining what is difficult or obscure on the one hand, or stressing points of character, style or plot on the other. Revision questions will be set on each act or group of chapters to test the student's careful application to the text of the prescribed book.

The second section of each of these study aids will consist of a critical examination of the author's art. This will cover such major elements as characterization, style, structure, setting, theme(s) or any other aspect of the book which the editor considers needs close study. The paramount aim is to send the student back to the text. Each study aid will include a series of general questions which require a detailed knowledge of the set book; the first of these questions will have notes by the editor of what *might* be included in a written answer. A short list of books considered useful as background reading for the student will be provided at the end.

Graham Handley.

The author and his work

Bill Naughton was born in County Mayo, Ireland in 1910. His family moved to Bolton, Lancashire in 1914, where his father worked as a coal-miner. During his early life in Bolton, Bill Naughton was subjected to the rigours of a Catholic education, which left him wondering at the disparity between the Christian ideals of the school and the frequent beatings inflicted on the pupils.

Bill Naughton's ambition to be a writer did not begin to reach fulfilment until 1943, when he had a short story printed in the *Evening Standard*. At the time he was working as a lorry driver in London – he was a conscientious objector during the war – and had joined the Peace Pledge Union. By 1945, Bill Naughton was beginning to become established as a writer, having had stories broadcast by the BBC. As well as producing short stories and radio scripts, Bill Naughton also wrote children's fiction, screenplays and some autobiographical work. He became famous in the 1960s for his domestic dramas portraying regional life. His first play *All in Good Time*, about wedding-night rituals in Bolton, was performed in 1963.

Much of the richness and understanding of working-class life which is apparent in *Spring and Port Wine* derives from his recall of his early experiences whilst growing to adulthood in Bolton, where he lived with his wife and family, before moving to London during the Second World War. His most famous story, *Alfie*, which charts the life of an amoral, promiscuous young man in London during the 1960s, was made into a popular film, starring Michael Caine. *Spring and Port Wine* was first published in 1957, entitled *My Flesh, My Blood*. Bill Naughton revised and rewrote the work and it was first performed, in its present form and bearing its present title, in 1965 at the Mermaid Theatre in London.

Literary terms used in these notes

Aphorism   A pithy, often proverbial saying, embodying a general truth.

Comedy   A play with a happy ending. It will provoke laughter, but the events of the drama may well have serious implications. The presiding impetus of these events will be towards final reconciliation of conflicting forces. It will be good-natured in tone, concentrating on human foibles and fallibilities, rather than wickedness.

Dramatic Irony   Occurs when a character speaks words, the full significance of which he does not realize. The audience, who are in full possession of the facts, *do* appreciate the significance of the character's words.

Imagery   Any figurative use of language. 'Word-pictures', which utilize the mind's capacity to respond emotionally to an idea which is evoked by the words.

Irony   Occurs when the real meaning of what is expressed is at variance with what appears to be said, i.e. the surface meaning is in conflict with the true significance of the words in the play. Or when a character does not realize the true significance of its utterance. Sometimes events unfold in a manner which the character least expects – the so-called 'Irony of Fate'.

Symbolism   Occurs when an object has the power to arouse thoughts and feelings in an audience, which may have particular relevance to the theme of the play. Sometimes an episode in the play possesses this power.

Structure and plot

The plot of *Spring and Port Wine* is simple and strong. In Act I
we see the seeds of dissension being sown – it is Friday
evening. Daisy attempts to account for the money she has
spent, and then puts herself in debt again to lend money to
Betsy Jane. Hilda's refusal to eat her evening meal is the
catalyst for the family to question Rafe's authority and to
challenge his attitude towards them. By Act II Scene 1
(Sunday teatime) the main issues in the play are unresolved
and relationships deteriorate culminating in the humiliation
of Wilfred and the departure of Hilda. Act II Scene 2 briefly
underlines Hilda's determination to leave and describes
Daisy's attempt to rob Rafe's cash-box; suspense is further
heightened by the pawning of Rafe's overcoat, which he
must surely discover. Act II Scene 3 deals with the enlighten-
ment of Rafe and the re-establishing of his relationship with
Daisy, which acts as a prelude to the reuniting of the whole
family. Seen in its entirety, the plot follows the traditional
comic pattern: the status quo is interrupted by discord;
disruption and potential disaster arise because of misunder-
standing; but the underlying goodness in human nature
triumphs – a new order, better than the old, is established.

In order that harmony may be restored, we are invited to
see the characters in a balanced light: if they have faults they
are countered by their innate goodness of heart. There are no
villains in the play. Thus, as well as displaying some of the
traits of a bullying tyrant, Rafe is also a caring and loving
father. Also, we see that Daisy's innate goodness counter-
acts, and undoes, the worst effects of Rafe's bullying.

The conflict in the play is heightened not because of
the differences in character between Rafe and Hilda, but

because they share a stubbornness, which will not permit them to back down. Furthermore, the underlying sense of pattern in the relationships of the Cromptons is emphasized because the children are shown to share the characteristics of their parents. Wilfred, for example, seems closest to his mother and reveals his sympathetic nature when he attempts to protect Hilda from having to eat the herring.

The overall movement towards reconciliation is also apparent in the way the incidental moments of disruption are succeeded by moments of reconciliation: characteristically, scenes end in tension, which is relieved by calm at the start of the next scene. This sequence is 'reassuring' for the audience and holds out the promise of a grand reconciliation at the end of the play.

Act summaries, critical commentaries, textual notes and revision questions

Act I pages 1–10

The play opens with Florence helping her mother with her arithmetic. Daisy is responsible for the weekly management of the family finances. Clearly, Rafe, Daisy's husband, is something of a stickler, and his requirement that every penny of his pay packet be accounted for puts a considerable strain upon his wife, who must indulge in borrowing and petty subterfuges in order to make the books balance. Florence lends her mother a pound. Daisy's problems are compounded by the arrival of Betsy Jane, who asks for a loan of five pounds. Daisy's good-natured generosity in offering Betsy Jane some money is rewarded by a tongue-lashing from her slatternly neighbour, who is contemptuous of her subservience to Rafe; Daisy is accused of lacking pride and independence. Despite her shock at learning that she has become a subject of gossip, Daisy asks her younger son, Wilfred, to lend her five pounds – so that she can satisfy Betsy Jane. On receiving her money, Betsy Jane regrets her outburst. Harold, Daisy's elder son, arrives home: his 'irresponsibility' is established by his habits of smoking and betting – both contrary to his father's wishes. When Hilda arrives home from work, she is evidently slightly tipsy. Hilda has a boyfriend who has neglected to write to her and she has unaccountably lost her taste for herrings. Harold expresses some defiance of his father, but his resolve evaporates as he catches sight of Rafe's approach.

Commentary

Amusingly and deftly, Bill Naughton establishes the characters and themes of his play. Daisy is under the thumb of her husband: Rafe's requirement that every penny be accounted for leads her into a round of borrowings and petty subterfuges. By such means, she hopes to keep the peace in the family and avert her husband's disapproval. But Daisy is not a good manager: her innate generosity leads her into further financial difficulties, which can only be retrieved by borrowing from her children. Daisy is unselfish but she is on a financial treadmill; she will, however, hear no word against her husband, whom she clearly respects and loves. It is ironic that the first intimations of her subservience should be brought to her attention by Betsy Jane – a good-natured, if messy and parasitical neighbour, who herself is unwittingly dominated by her 'chap'. Betsy Jane, whose life is chaotic, perceives that the overt calm and order of the Cromptons is maintained at the expense of Daisy's pride and independence. This is a harsh judgement, but it embodies enough truth to disturb Daisy's self-possession. At this stage in the play, Daisy's pride resides in the maintenance of an ordered home, the bringing up of her children and the pacification of Rafe.

Daisy's children all feel affection for their mother and they are willing to aid her in her difficulties: even Harold parts with his money for her sake. Obviously, she has earned their loyalty and love. Indeed, she has created such a secure environment that Florence is reluctant to strike out on her own and face her own responsibilities as a home-builder. Harold, despite his defiance of his father, is still resident in the family home, and Wilfrid, the 'baby' of the family, is not yet ready for the outside world. Only Hilda seems prepared to support her assertion of self hood with actions: she refuses her herring merely because she has 'gone off 'em' (a statement which earns a jibe from Harold, who says that she is 'getting above herself'). Hilda's independence of spirit is established as soon as she appears: her clothing is bright and individualistic, her manner reveals slight intoxication.

Obviously, the opening of the play hints at issues which are later to become important: the Crompton family is growing up; the children are beginning to assert their independence – thus we are led to focus on the relationship between parents and children, and we are shortly to become involved in their efforts to leave a secure, but stifling environment. At the same time, we are also involved in the development of Daisy, as she sheds her subservience to Rafe and the needs of her family – to discover a new pride and independence in her relationship with her husband. This process of self-discovery is conducted against the background of a changing world: the old values are being questioned and sifted. Naughton still finds much to cherish in the old ways and we are not invited to mock the tribalism and loyalties traditionally associated with North-Country ways.

Exploration of these (and other) themes lies in the future, and, although they are weighty issues, Bill Naughton's handling of them is essentially comic: the underlying respect which the characters feel for each other, and the good-natured banter keep the tone light.

The characters are strongly differentiated, although they all spring from the same mould: the quiet, shy Wilfred contrasts with his louder, impertinent brother. Similarly, the staid Florence is contrasted with the more lively, erratic Hilda. Although we hear much about Rafe, Naughton delays his appearance – thus suspense is aroused.

The living-room . . . The setting remains constant throughout the play. Naughton's stage-direction suggests a well-ordered household.

seemingly A tell-tale word. The underlying stresses are shortly to be revealed.

usual time There is a great emphasis on routine in the Crompton household: any slight deviation is noticed.

six pounds . . . ha'penny Daisy counts in pounds and shillings (1 shilling = 5p). The play was written before the metrication of money.

father's head for sums The children of the Cromptons resemble their parents – despite ostensible differences.

make them all tally i.e. make the accounts balance: Rafe expects to find that Daisy's expenditure is consistent with her income.

an honest ring i.e. an honest appearance. It is becoming clear that Daisy to some extent has become accustomed to living by appearances – in order to pacify her husband. Ironically, at the end of the play we learn that Rafe has known all along about his wife's petty subterfuges over money.

done a bunk Daisy has a sense of humour – but the question of the children (and Rafe) leaving home is to become a serious issue later in the play.

for your dad's peace of mind True, but it is also for Daisy's peace of mind, and the harmony of the whole household.

out of the red Out of debt.

Three nights a week of Arthur Florence is *playing* the fiancée: she has not faced the reality of marriage. Strictly speaking, she is evading her responsibilities to Arthur, preferring to remain cocooned in her family.

herrings for tea A casual reference which introduces an important element in the play: Hilda's refusal to eat her herring precipitates a crisis in the Crompton family.

fish of a Friday A suggestion of Rafe's religious temperament.

have got to like it Betsy Jane has a shrewd understanding of the order of things.

High Church Leaning towards Roman Catholicism.

eddicated Educated.

Baptists i.e. Non-Conformist: 'Low Church'.

Yon chap will murder me Despite her assertions to the contrary, Betsy Jane is dominated by her husband.

barefaced lie Daisy has 'forgotten' her earlier conversation with Florence: eight and six was 'paid' to a non-existent window cleaner. Daisy, of course, finds it difficult to speak an untruth to Rafe, but she is able to countenance a falsified account-book.

Money runs the house There is an element of truth in this statement.

we don't owe a halfpenny Daisy takes pride in the Crompton lack of hire-purchase debts.

my neighbours talk . . . behind my back Daisy is outraged by this outsider's perception of her situation.

all your life is a flaming lie Betsy Jane exaggerates, but again there is an element of truth here. There is a sense in which Daisy has settled for harmony in the house – at the expense of her pride; she has allowed herself to become a slave to Rafe's rigidities; she will tell falsehoods in order to avoid Rafe's disapproval.

What he doesn't know . . . Wilfred espouses his mother's philosophy.

I've just heard a bit of truth Daisy cannot dismiss Betsy Jane's earlier remarks about her lack of pride and independence.

grab the sink i.e. to have a wash.

squire A jocular form of address.

sluice Wash.

Egyptians i.e. a particularly good quality cotton.

a bit of a do i.e. a celebration.

one born i.e. 'There's a fool born every minute.' Proverbial.

not the only reason Harold suspects that many brides are pregnant! A cynical observation, which later becomes relevant when it is suspected that Hilda may be pregnant.

Airwick A deodorizing agent.

I'll tell him where he gets off Brave words which are not apparent when Rafe actually arrives!

Co-op A reference to the Co-operative Wholesale Society – a retail outlet which sells basic commodities and pays a share of the profits to its customers.

footing A traditional Lancashire celebration – explained a little later.

Boer War i.e. a long time ago. The Boer War took place at the turn of the century, when supposedly Daisy was a young woman!

Springtime orgies An obviously ironical remark, but it is interesting that Hilda, although she has only just arrived, is associated with ideas of tipsiness, springtime and abandon. Her role in the play is thus anticipated: she is to be instrumental in loosening the shackles of tradition, habit and deceit which are prevalent in the Crompton family.

Hymns The society of which Naughton writes has not lost sight of the old values and traditions – hence the incongruity.

I've gone off 'em Hilda's change of taste suggests to Daisy that her daughter may be pregnant.

getting above herself Hilda's assertion of personal preference is remarkable in the context of the Crompton household.

your cat Our attention is drawn to a creature which is to play a part later in the drama.

Beaujolais A red wine from France.

flapping a paper about A comic moment as Harold's defiance evaporates in this frenzied attempt to conceal his smoking.

Act I pages 11–19

Rafe arrives home from work: he is clearly master of the house. Daisy will soon have his tea ready, and Florence brings his slippers. The Crompton children dutifully hand over portions of their pay-packets: some of the money is saved and put into Rafe's strong-box (he alone possesses the key) – the remainder is passed on to Daisy, for housekeeping. Rafe inspects Daisy's account book and pronounces himself satisfied. Harold's attempt to keep back a pound for himself is to no avail.

Tea is prepared and, after Rafe has taken his place at the head of the table, the main course – herrings – is produced. The harmony of the meal is shattered by Hilda, who refuses to eat her herring. Rafe takes charge and tells Hilda that she cannot leave the table. Rafe then relates a brief history of the Hunger Marches; and tells the story of a period in his own life when he knew unemployment and hardship. Hilda is unmoved by these examples of need. The herring is to be put on one side and Hilda is told that she will be served it for every meal (and nothing else), until she decides that she will eat it. After issuing these instructions, Rafe leaves to prepare for his Union meeting.

Commentary

The focus of the play now shifts to Rafe, as Bill Naughton develops his character. He is not the simple tyrant we may have been led to expect. It is true that he seeks to dominate Daisy and his children. He believes that his will should be law; but he also possesses endearing qualities which give him humanity and stature. We can now see why Daisy loves and respects her husband. Rafe is clearly a product of his harsh North-Country background: he has been brought up to revere the 'old virtues' – he professes to admire truth, he loves poetry and beauty, he is impatient of bad manners. His experience of life has taught him that food which is put on the table should be eaten, and not abandoned for a whim. But for all his apparent sensitivity, he is a dogmatic man – and often given to sententious speech, which reveals an essential insensitivity to the needs of others in their own particular situations. He believes in principles, so long as they are his principles; he believes that he has the god-given right to determine the principles and behaviour of others. Of course, a father may to some extent determine the behaviour of his children; but Rafe does not perceive that Hilda is no longer a child.

Although Rafe obviously cares for his wife and family, he lacks the understanding heart which would enable him to see the cruelty in his treatment of Hilda; fortunately, his harshness is balanced by the softness of Daisy and Wilfred, who will see to it that Hilda does not starve. Florence tends to side unequivocally with her father; Harold becomes openly more contemptuous of him.

The immediate cause of the conflict – a mere herring – preserves the element of comedy, amidst the strongly-held opinions and raw emotions. Bill Naughton understands that trivialities often bring to the surface underlying tensions within a family setting. The herring is a catalyst whereby these tensions in the family will be brought to a crisis, although at this stage no one grasps precisely how serious the conflict will become. Before it is settled, all the characters come to a deeper understanding of themselves and their relationships with each other; it will be a painful process for some. Daisy's optimism that they will 'get over it' is correct, but much suffering precedes the happy ending of the play.

a bit of peace An ironic remark in the light of what is to ensue.

engine Refers to the engines which drive the machinery in the mill.

family Bible Rafe's religious spirit is soon established.

'When I do count the clock . . .' Shakespeare, Sonnet XII. The theme that time is passing, and good things are in a state of decay, mirrors Rafe's feelings about the 'modern' world. ['Sable' = dark]

'Which erst . . .' Harold's ability to quote the line (and his mime) indicates that he has heard the piece many times before. ['erst' = formerly]

I think so . . . Daisy avoids telling a 'barefaced' lie.

'Neither a borrower . . .' Rafe quotes from Polonius's advice to Laertes in *Hamlet*.

Sauce tartare Florence pretentiously uses the correct French word order.

piquant Sharp-tasting.

I'm entitled to some choice This remark encapsulates Hilda's attitude: essentially it is a question of her free will. The immediate cause of dissension (the herring) is trivial.

You'll do nothing of the sort Rafe is not a man to compromise.

there's nobody taking me for granted It has become a personal matter: a clash of wills.

Hunger Marchers Refers to the famous march of unemployed ship-builders from Clydeside to London – in the early 1930s. Rafe's story of the Hunger Marchers and his own hardship is movingly told and ensures that his treatment of Hilda is given a reason; thus we are forced to sympathize with both characters. Hilda has the right to choose what she will eat; but Rafe is no unthinking, heartless monster.

tenter Tender, minder.

young people are today . . . The traditional lament of the older generation.

until she eats it Again, no compromise in Rafe. He is right about the undesirability of wasting food, but his treatment of Hilda lacks magnanimity – which should outweigh adherence to this principle.

take him away in the yellow cab i.e. to the 'madhouse'.

it's over a principle Instinctively, Florence perceives the real issue – it's a question of order, or, more precisely, does Rafe's order rule? If he gives way to Hilda, then Florence believes the Crompton household will become a free-for-all, where chaos reigns.

the only one in the house Hilda believes that other people have a right to their tastes and opinions.

butty Sandwich.

Bespoke Tailors i.e. they make clothes to order, as distinct from cheaper tailors, who sell ready-made clothes.

weskit Waist-coat.

Act I pages 20–27

The parcel, which has arrived for Rafe, contains an expensive overcoat. Harold, in particular, is outraged that his father can spend thirty-two guineas on a coat, but Daisy unselfishly defends her husband. Rafe takes great pride in his new acquisition: it is made from fine cloth and represents good value for money.

Arthur, Florence's fiancé, arrives with the news that his boss, Mr Aspinall, is about to retire – thus leaving open the possibility of Arthur's promotion to works manager. But Aspinall will only grant the position to a married man, whom he believes will manifest the required stability of character. The promotion is Arthur's, provided that Florence agrees to marry him – in the very near future. There should be no problem – after all, Florence and Arthur have been engaged for a year! However, Rafe immediately raises objections to his daughter's marriage: he is particularly angered that Aspinall should presume to dictate in such matters; he can remember a time when Aspinall was a mere tinker. Arthur outlines all the fringe benefits that will accrue to him as a works manager, but Rafe remains adamant: he did not bring up his daughter to have her marriage date determined by a person whom he holds in contempt. Rafe departs for his Union meeting.

Commentary

The underlying tensions in the Crompton family are once more exposed, this time by Rafe's purchase of an expensive overcoat: Harold, Hilda and Wilfred regard it as a selfish extravagance. Florence, typically, aligns herself with her father and Daisy cannot see any harm in the purchase. Rafe is unashamed, and justifies himself on grounds of need, and the quality of the cloth. Of course, there is no reason why Rafe should not buy the coat – the significance of the episode is that even such an everyday action, by this stage, is a cause of dissension and animosity directed against Rafe. Furthermore, the coat has an importance which emerges later: Bill Naughton skilfully incorporates it into the plotting of his play as it moves towards its climax.

Arthur's improved prospects introduce more tension into the drama. First, Florence now has to make a decision about marriage – an event which she has preferred to keep in the background of her life. Secondly, Rafe's opposition to the marriage is absolute. Once again, the family takes sides: Daisy, Hilda, Harold and Wilfred all believe that the marriage represents an opportunity for Florence to better herself. Ironically, only Florence seems to support her father, but perhaps her reticence, whilst others comment, may indicate a division in her own mind. Certainly, she faces a dilemma not dissimilar in essence to that of Hilda: should she subscribe to her father's authority, or should she exercise a choice which goes against him? It is not a straightforward matter: Rafe's reasons for opposing the marriage on Aspinall's terms are reasonable, although one suspects that they are partly motivated by sheer snobbery. Also, of course, Florence is required to make an adult decision which will affect the future course of her life. It must be tempting simply to remain in the security of home rather than face the challenge of forging a permanent relationship with Arthur. Bill Naughton sensitively explores the situation and does not permit us to make a facile decision on the point at issue; much of what Rafe says makes sense, but perhaps we are invited to side with Daisy, whose pragmatic view carries much weight. It would be a mistake to see her as entirely subservient to Rafe; she opposed him over Hilda's herring, and now she is quick to see the advantages in Florence's marriage – and she is not afraid to state her views.

Chelsea boots Ankle-length boots, very fashionable at the time.

Knots . . . unfastened Rafe has a proverbial utterance for all occasions. This one might be taken to refer to the play as a whole: the Cromptons will have a knot to unfasten – if they are to survive as a family, without becoming cut off from one another.

(aside) one sneeze . . . naked Harold has not the courage to state his opinions openly.

I can't think what he wants Florence's off-hand reaction to Arthur's arrival contrasts with the spontaneous welcome he receives from Hilda.

I wish you had one like it Florence idolizes her father; she is not yet ready to form a loving relationship with Arthur.

gradely Lancashire dialect: 'fine', 'grand'.

So it will. Rafe does not realize that Harold is being sarcastic.

tea Traditionally a more substantial meal in the North of England than in the South.

Oh . . . middlin' The inconsequential, awkward small-talk indicates that Arthur has something important to say. [middlin' = not bad]

a nice fried herring Harold cannot resist this provocative remark!

if me and your Florence would get wed Aspinall's offer will force Florence to come to a decision about marriage.

marry at the bidding of a tinker This remark indicates Rafe's snobbery and contrasts with some of his more reasonable objections to Florence's marriage. Essentially, of course, it has become a personal matter: will Florence follow her own best interests, or will she obey her father? She, like Hilda, is now confronted with a choice.

let a wife of mine go out to work A characteristically old-fashioned attitude, but Rafe's objections to Aspinall's terms are not unreasonable: there is something presumptuous in requiring Arthur to be married, and the material inducements smack of bribery.

feudal Aspinall is behaving like a medieval lord of the manor.

mithered Confused, muddled. Rafe's arguments have had their effect.

Good night, everybody Although Rafe's arguments have been powerful, he leaves the house an isolated figure. Ironically, only Florence seems to support him, but she has been silent during much of the debate.

shuttance Riddance.

Act I pages 28–34

Arthur feels that Harold and Wilfred are cowardly in front of their father, although he admits that he did not put his own case satisfactorily. Whilst not actually rejecting Arthur, Florence refuses to be rushed into matrimony. Hilda is critical of Florence because she appears to support her father. A few moments later Hilda bursts into tears, in response to some heavy-handed teasing about her failed love-affair with Donald. Arthur comforts Hilda by putting his arm around her. Daisy urges Florence to give Arthur an answer; Harold is confident that Florence will refuse him, and that Arthur may well marry Hilda.

Left alone with Arthur, Florence cannot forbear mentioning that he seemed too assiduous in his comforting of Hilda. Arthur admits that he likes Hilda, but states unequivocally that he loves Florence. Inspired by this declaration, Florence embraces Arthur passionately. This proceeding is witnessed by Hilda, Daisy and Rafe. The curtain falls.

Commentary

Hilda's refusal to bow to her father's wishes and eat the herring brought about a crisis in the family. Now, Arthur precipitates a further questioning of Rafe's authority. Initially, it seems that Florence will side with her father and turn down Arthur's proposal. Stimulated by jealousy and Arthur's declaration of love, however, Florence decides to marry him and seals her intention with a passionate embrace. Thus Rafe, in opposing the match, now finds himself even more isolated from his family, and his authority over his children is very much in doubt. Daisy, as ever, is torn both ways: she does not waver in her love for Rafe, but this devotion is in conflict with what she believes is best for her children. Daisy's predicament is underlined by Harold, who observes that she is going 'humpbacked . . . with worry'.

I'll show you Hilda is a girl of spirit.
I'm used to it Daisy betrays her weariness by this remark.
double deckers i.e. sandwiches.
has to carry the can This statement is true. Daisy has to bear the strain of her divided loyalties – to Rafe and to her children.
he honestly cares Wilfred perceives that Rafe's strictness is an aspect of caring.
I don't fancy living on my own Harold cannot feel that his home is so bad, otherwise he would respond differently to Arthur's suggestion that he find a place of his own.
Wanderers i.e. Bolton Wanderers Football Club.
'Allan Water' A ballad. Music and song play an important part in the life of the Cromptons. It derives from Rafe, who is himself influenced by the tradition of North-Country musicality. Bill Naughton uses music and song to underline the mood of a scene.
Have your cry out Arthur often shows a practical wisdom and sympathy.

I'm sorry Harold realizes that he has gone too far; he, too, has a sympathetic side to his nature.

don't go without your answer Bill Naughton increases the dramatic tension as the Act draws to a conclusion.

more fond of her Florence is jealous of Hilda.

embrace passionately Florence has made her commitment.

the Curtain falls A dramatic moment, which propels us forward into Act II: how will Rafe react to Florence's defiance of his expressed wish?

Revision questions on Act I

1 Describe the attitude of the Crompton children towards their father.

2 What are your first impressions of Rafe?

3 Show how Daisy endeavours to keep the peace in her family.

4 What evidence is there that Hilda resembles her father?

5 What does Rafe's description of the Hunger Marchers contribute towards your understanding of his character?

6 How far do you agree with Rafe in his objections to the marriage of Arthur and Florence?

7 Do you think that Rafe has the right to expect obedience from his children?

8 Do you find it convincing that such a crisis arises from Hilda's refusal to eat a herring?

9 Show how Bill Naughton maintains the tension during this long Act.

10 What contribution do the interventions of Harold make during the Act?

Act II Scene 1 pages 35–49

It is Sunday teatime. Betsy Jane has not paid her debt to Daisy. Wilfred is short of money and so Daisy has to pay him back from her current housekeeping money. The herring issue has not yet been resolved. Hilda decides that she will eat the entire herring (although it is now 'high') in order to restore peace in the home. Daisy tells her that Rafe will not force her to eat the fish – his honour will be satisfied if Hilda merely shows willing. Hilda understands this, but intends to humiliate her father by refusing to accept his magnanimity: she will eat 'the lot'; Rafe will be made to suffer as he watches the proceedings. Rafe returns and confirms, as Daisy predicted, that he will feel he has won if Hilda makes only a move to eat the herring; he does not intend to force her to eat it, but he will not be 'bested' in a trial of wills. Daisy is much saddened that family life has become a battle.

But Wilfred has decided to take matters into his own hands: during a family sing-song, he sneaks the cat out of the room and gives it the herring. When the herring is not produced at teatime, Rafe is furious: he does not believe that the cat removed the fish from the plate in the kitchen of its own volition. An 'inquisition' is conducted and by a process of elimination Wilfred stands accused, but he cannot bring himself to admit his guilt; he becomes increasingly distraught as his father steps up the pressure upon him to confess. Finally, on being asked to declare his innocence whilst holding the Bible, he collapses in a dead faint. Daisy ministers to Wilfred, whilst Hilda, who has been sickened by her father's callous behaviour, quits the house. Now that the truth has been revealed, Rafe is satisfied and his anger subsides – but he is roundly rebuked for his conduct by Arthur, who regards his behaviour as tyrannical. Arthur asks Florence to leave the house with him. She must decide now. With a sob, Florence leaves with Arthur, thus defying her father's wishes.

Commentary

As the Act opens, little seems to have changed, but it is the calm before the storm. Both Daisy and Wilfred respect Rafe's fixity of purpose, whilst at the same time sympathizing with Hilda. By the end of the Act, two contentious issues are settled (Hilda's herring and Florence's marriage). It is a painful process.

Despite the obvious differences of age and temperament, Hilda has inherited her father's stubbornness: she also reveals a shrewd understanding of his psychology, as she outlines her plan to discomfort her father by consuming the entire herring. A moment or two later, Rafe explains that it is not his intention that the herring should be eaten: Hilda merely has to 'show willing'. He is simply concerned not to be 'bested'. In both these instances, Daisy is the recipient of the information: therefore she has the role of confidante to both of the antagonistic parties. It must weary her to see her two loved ones playing these 'games'. Indeed, it is apparent that, like many families, the Cromptons have evolved strategies and deceptions by means of which they conduct their family affairs. Daisy is not exempt: she pretends to be able to manage the family budget. Ironically, many of these deceptions are devised to pacify Rafe's overriding desire for truth and probity in all his dealings. Later, however, we learn that Rafe himself has pretended to go along with Daisy's deceptions. It has all become very complicated; the family needs a crisis and disruption so that it may achieve a new honesty and understanding of its relationships.

Disruption is not long in coming: Rafe's reaction to Wilfred's well-intended subterfuge is terrifying and inevitable; his adherence to principle (at all costs) results in his son's breakdown and the departure of Hilda and Florence. We see here how Rafe's Old Testament values, devoid of human understanding, can wreak havoc in the family. Rafe is not an insensitive man: he has a sentimental attachment to music and poetry; after his own fashion, he deeply loves his family, but he cannot yet perceive how horribly destructive adherence to abstract principle may be when it is untempered by love and forgiveness. He should have been able to understand that Wilfred's dishonesty sprang from a desire to protect his sister and preserve the harmony of the family. Unfortunately, he is driven by his desire for 'the truth', and his need not to be bested – it is not easy to assess which feeling predominates.

But all is not negative. When Arthur confronts him with some home-truths at the end of the scene, Rafe lets him have his say and states that he is 'learning'. Despite the troubles which beset the Cromptons during the play, Bill Naughton reminds us frequently that they have the latent capacity to love and understand one another. The play is a comedy: the potential for a happy ending is never entirely lost from sight.

Sunday, teatime . . . table Despite the events of the first Act nothing, outwardly, seems to have changed. There is a feeling of normality.

come in Pay back.

a very dodgy week-end This is something of an understatement.

Yorkshire Yorkshire pudding.

Epsom Salts A proprietary laxative.

high Strong-smelling.

Summat Something.

He hardly touched his meat Wilfred's sensitive nature could not let him eat meat which had been denied his sister.

constitutional A walk (for the sake of his health).

act as a buffer Precisely defines Daisy's position in the family.

Poor dad . . . He'd make two of you Daisy's respect for Rafe is unabated.

codding 'Kidding', joking.

I'll whip that herring away Ironically, Rafe's plan to resolve the issue is in conflict with Hilda's plan to eat the entire herring.

I never intended . . . eat it Rafe has been indulging in strategy – it would have been better if he had been more straightforward.

If your children once beat you Indicative that Rafe sees family life in terms of conflict. A fundamental contrast with Daisy who deplores the idea that bringing up a family should be a 'battle'.

shared a world in common Of thematic relevance: it is true that the Crompton children have been brought up during a period of unprecedented change. Thus the conflict between generations is inevitably heightened.

Handel G. F. Handel (1685–1750). Composer of the famous 'Largo' Oratorio. Rafe's love of poetry, music and song (and the English countryside) makes him a 'rounded' character and enhances our sympathy for him.

the singing is moving As they gather round the piano to sing the 'Largo', the harmony of the family is emphasized. In the midst of uncertainty about the future it is a hopeful sign.

carrying the cat and the herring A comic moment, but our pleasure in it is modified by the knowledge that Wilfred's good intentions cut across the plans of Rafe and Hilda.

Green boughs . . . laid A moment of serenity before the storm; Bill Naughton regulates his audience's feelings in masterly fashion.

King of Kings From Handel's 'Messiah' (The 'Hallelujah Chorus').

moral decay Characteristically, Rafe sees the world in black and white terms.

forgotten something The critical moment has arrived; tension has mounted during the previous dialogue.

returns holding the remains of the herring A comic and threatening moment.

No cat of mine A ludicrous statement – Rafe supposes that even the cat knows its place!

It's an inquest on the truth The mood of the scene has changed dramatically.

Me? Why should I? Wilfred's evasions are pathetic.

Don't press him too far Everyone, apart from Rafe, can see that his bullying persecution of Wilfred is causing the lad immense suffering. Rafe's obsession with 'the truth' has led him to forget his common humanity. It is a failure of imagination.

I'll never come back . . . prison Hilda is outraged by what she has witnessed – she determines to leave. In contrast, Daisy's concern is to revive Wilfred, rather than indulge in recriminations; of course, there is no escape route open to her.

hang fire Hold back.

The truth was staring you in the face Arthur defines Rafe's sin against Wilfred: he set himself up as God, allowing his desire for truth to override Christian charity.

ARTHUR *takes her* **(Florence)** *and exits* Rafe reaps the consequences of his actions – his two daughters have left the house.

Revision questions on Act II Scene 1

1 Explain how Hilda plans to 'defeat' her father over the herring.

2 What does this scene contribute towards your understanding of Rafe and Daisy?

3 Discuss the importance to the play of Wilfred's attempt to resolve the herring-issue, by feeding it to the cat.

4 What is the significance of Arthur's confrontation with Rafe at the end of the scene?

5 Why do you think Florence behaves as she does at the final moment of this scene?

Act II Scene 2 pages 49–54

After her hasty exit, Hilda ventured no further than the local canal, where she was found by Betsy Jane's husband. She spent the night under Betsy Jane's roof. Nonetheless, Hilda insists that she intends to leave home and go to London, where she hopes to find a job. Daisy is understandably anxious about her pretty daughter arriving penniless in the wicked city. With the help of Betsy Jane, the lock of the desk where Rafe keeps his cash-box is picked, but Daisy cannot bring herself to allow the box itself to be prised open. In desperation, Daisy fetches Rafe's new overcoat and asks that Betsy Jane pawn it for her. Naturally, Daisy hopes that she will be able to redeem the coat before Rafe discovers its loss.

Commentary

Wilfred, Florence and Hilda have all performed acts in defiance of Rafe; now it is Daisy's turn. She is driven to this deed because she cannot let her daughter venture penniless to London: Hilda's self-assertion over the herring has precipitated a chain reaction of defiance of Rafe's authority. When Daisy reluctantly permits Betsy Jane to pick the lock of the desk, she knows that she must be found out: previously she has managed to cover up her indiscretions and she has avoided barefaced denial of her husband's wishes. Thus we have reached a crucial moment in the play: when Rafe discovers Daisy's 'crime', his isolation will be total; the survival of the family unit will be gravely threatened. The pawning of the overcoat represents a final attempt to conceal her 'indiscretions': but it, too, is an action fraught with danger.

At last, Daisy has taken a stand – instead of constantly seeking to compromise – although, it must be added that these compromises were often undertaken for unselfish reasons. It is a measure of the pass to which things have come that Daisy cannot bring herself to confront Rafe openly with the situation: she is frightened, and cannot trust her husband.

Money has always been a source of contention in the Crompton family and it has been a constant worry for Daisy, as she concealed her inability to manage the family finances. It is appropriate, therefore, that the crisis focuses upon the cash-box. The attempt to break into 'the holy of holies' represents an assault upon one of the time-honoured rituals

of the family – it cannot be violated without serious consequences.

Betsy Jane emerges from this scene as more than simply a
slatternly scrounger: she is not principled about money; nor
is she particularly solicitous of the truth; but she possesses a
rough and ready good nature, which leads her to giving
Hilda a bed for the night and to lend her skills to Daisy in
picking the lock of the desk. Betsy Jane is confident that it is
'a man's world' – but she does her best, by subterfuge, to
redress the balance.

'Housewives' Choice' A popular radio record request show of
the time. The arrival of Betsy Jane effectively lowers the tension
after the traumas of the previous scene. The audience needs a
'rest'!
clannish Close-knit, secretive.
You stick together A positive sign.
Your Hilda . . . say a word Betsy Jane has deliberately
withheld the information that Hilda spent the night with her
family.
Open confession . . . soul Another home-truth, of relevance to
the Cromptons. Betsy Jane is, of course, unaware of this
significance – an example of dramatic irony.
boasting about my dad Indicates the depth of the relationship
between father and daughter. This pride needs to be
rediscovered.
hob A ledge at the side of a fireplace, on which a kettle may be
boiled.
nature of things Another positive, hopeful observation.
felt sick this morning Daisy again wonders if Hilda may be
pregnant.
never bears grudges There is a fund of goodness upon which
the family may draw – when the time is ripe.
something worse Daisy again alludes to her suspicion that
Hilda may be pregnant.
without money A presiding problem in the play.
pimps Men who live upon the earnings of prostitutes.
Put it back! Daisy has allowed herself to be lured into an act of
outright defiance of Rafe.

Houdini The celebrated American escapologist.
the holy of holies More dramatic irony – it *is* the holy of holies.
I could get round it somehow Daisy seeks to escape into her
  old ways, but this time there can be no compromise – the deed
  has been done.
pop it Pawn it.

Revision questions on Act II Scene 2

1 Outline the importance of Betsy Jane during this scene.

2 Why do you think that Hilda did not go directly to
London?

3 Daisy puts up with Rafe because he is 'genuine'. What
does she mean by this? Is Rafe entirely genuine?

4 Why does Daisy draw back from breaking open the
cash-box? What is the significance of the cash-box to the
Cromptons?

5 Why does Daisy permit Betsy Jane to pawn Rafe's
overcoat?

Act II Scene 3 pages 55–63

Betsy Jane has managed to raise some money by pawning
Rafe's overcoat. In an effort to get Rafe out of the house
before the return of Florence and Hilda to collect their
possessions, Harold suggests that he should attend a per-
formance of Handel's 'Messiah'. Rafe agrees to go, but much
to Daisy's consternation, he is persuaded by Wilfred that he
should wear his new overcoat to the concert. Eventually,
Daisy is forced to confess that she has pawned the coat – and
also that she broke into Rafe's desk, in an attempt to get at
the money. Rafe, now made aware of the fear he has inspired
in the house, asks for Daisy's forgiveness, and, in a bid for
understanding, tells of his own unhappy childhood. As a

small boy, Rafe watched his mother desperately seeking to placate bailiffs; matters culminated in his mother's attempted suicide, which the young Rafe witnessed. In this manner, Rafe explains his detestation of money and his anxiety to save his own family from a life of deceit and debt.

Daisy shows her understanding of Rafe by embracing him; she asks that in future he will not expect his family to live up to impossibly high standards.

Commentary

The audience is on tenterhooks as the final scene opens: Rafe must surely find out about Daisy's 'sins'. Bill Naughton cleverly delays the moment of revelation, thereby fully exploiting the suspense which is inherent in the situation. Rafe seems strangely subdued, even defeated, by the storm which broke about him at the end of Act II, Scene 1: he even offers Daisy money – an ironic gesture, when we bear in mind that Daisy is already in possession of 'illicit' cash. Dramatic irony pervades the scene, deriving from the knowledge of Daisy's deceptions which the audience possesses; but, of course, this knowledge is denied to Wilfred, Harold and Rafe himself. The effect of this irony is to concentrate our attention on the suffering of Daisy, as the other characters unwittingly contribute towards her unmasking. Daisy's guilt is intensified because Rafe seems so reasonable and apologetic.

It is evident that Rafe has been severely shaken by the 'loss' of his daughters, but we still wonder how he will react when he hears about the violation of his desk and his pawned overcoat. Will the meekness remain, or will there be a tirade?

Daisy's confession is a prelude to a new honesty in the Crompton household: Rafe admits that he has always been aware of Daisy's financial incompetence. However, he had not realized that Daisy went in fear of him, this had not been his intention, rather he had sought to avoid causing her misery – another irony. Bill Naughton now deepens our sympathy for Rafe by having him tell of his unhappy childhood, when he witnessed the disintegration of his family and the near-suicide of his debt-ridden mother. Rafe had learned from this episode to despise money and fear its destructive power; he had therefore become determined that his family should avoid debt and the miseries and deceits associated with it. Unfortunately, his good intentions went astray because his obsessive adherence to truth and solvency led to his becoming divorced from a humane understanding of others' weaknesses. This revelation of Rafe's psychology is convincing and important: it is strategically placed in the play and provides impetus for the reconciliations which are about to take place – it is essential that we (and the other characters in the drama) should understand Rafe – if we are to forgive him for the tyrannical behaviour which was manifest in the earlier scenes. In more general terms, Bill Naughton is making a plea for the primacy of love, forgiveness and understanding over rigid pursuit of principle, even if the principle is soundly based.

The stage is now set for the final movement of the play: the Cromptons are not yet united, the children are still in disarray. Rafe's statement that he will 'think of some stroke' sustains our interest as the drama enters its final phase.

Chopin Nocturne A peaceful mood is set – unexpected, in the light of the previous scene, but perhaps it suggests harmony to come.

a man lost Bill Naughton has kept Rafe off-stage for an appreciable time. This remark prepares us for a changed man – perhaps Arthur's accusations at the end of Act 2, Scene 1 have had their effect? Has Daisy been precipitate in pawning the overcoat? Tension mounts.

it won't take much How much more does he need? One doubts his true resolve.

bureau A chest of drawers, used as a writing desk.

that's not tonight Rafe is wrong about a matter of fact, and admits it! For the first time? This is an indication of his disorientation.

not be around Rafe has lost his taste for confrontation.

needing some extra money Rafe's generosity provokes anxiety as he approaches the desk. Dramatic irony: Rafe does not realize the ominousness of his words.

striking up Beginning to play.

I think I will go Tension mounts as Rafe makes up his mind.

entering into a new world Dramatic irony: Rafe and the family are about to enter a 'new world'.

how about . . . new coat? Again, in seeking to be helpful, Wilfred precipitates a crisis. Bill Naughton manipulates suspense very effectively in this scene.

Let your dad please himself Daisy suffers – the price of her deception.

What do you mean? Daisy is guilty – she misinterprets this innocent remark.

Rafe exits Skilful dramatic writing: the suspense is maintained; Rafe himself discovers that the coat is missing; asks its whereabouts; the moment has come for Daisy to throw herself on Rafe's mercy in a theatrically effective embrace. It is the 'moment of truth'.

I haven't made you go in fear . . .? A time of realization for Rafe.

force . . . blind a man A key recognition of his own folly.

bailiffs Debt collectors, appointed by the law courts.

You never told me Why didn't Rafe tell his wife of these childhood experiences? In particular, of his mother's attempted suicide? Perhaps he felt that it would be asking for pity ('begging to be understood')?

I despise it This revelation of his past helps us to understand and feel sympathy for Rafe. Bill Naughton does not want us to take sides (we may have been tempted to do so earlier in the play). Instead, we are invited to participate in understanding his characters.

Act II Scene 3 pages 64–74

Rafe hands over the keys of his desk to Daisy; he goes upstairs when he hears his children approaching: he does not wish to face them yet, but it is apparent that he intends to devise a scheme to reunite the family. Florence and Arthur announce their impending marriage – by 'special licence'; Hilda has abandoned her plan to go to London, preferring instead to lodge with her friend, Betty Partington. Wilfred and Harold also intend to leave home. Betsy Jane arrives bearing two of the five pounds which she owes Daisy, but Daisy refuses to accept the money, on condition that Betsy Jane never asks her for another ha'penny. Betsy Jane retreats as she hears the approach of Rafe.

Rafe surprises Arthur by forgiving him for speaking his mind. Arthur and Florence are surprised that Rafe will no longer oppose their marriage; indeed, he intends to see that things are conducted properly.

Harold has to remind Wilfred of their intention to leave home! Rafe underlines his change of attitude by revealing that he envies his children their freedom to leave, and he tells Daisy that he has always known of her 'cooking the books'. He insists that she must now assume responsibility for the financial management of the home.

The 'new' Rafe worries the family – he does not appear to be himself – they are reluctant to see him leave the house in his present state of mind. Soon it becomes clear that Harold and Wilfred are not really ready to leave: they would miss the comforts and consolations of a good home. Harold suggests that they should all be reconciled and Arthur agrees that it would be a good idea to 'bury the hatchet'.

Rafe is unmoved, and still apparently determined to leave. However, in response to the pleas of Hilda, Wilfred and Harold, he changes his mind and decides to stay. Rafe and Daisy '*go to each other*'. Rafe orders that somebody puts the kettle on. The family is reunited.

Commentary

Rafe and Daisy have reached a new understanding of each other, but the Crompton family has yet to be reconciled: Rafe is alienated from his children. Arthur and Florence invite Daisy to come and live with them after they are married, but they all seem to have forgotten Rafe, until Daisy reminds them that he merits some consideration. Harold is content that his father should remain on his own in the house. Hilda, characteristically, is more sensitive to her father's needs, but the relationship between them has been sullied, and needs to be put right.

The onus is upon Rafe to re-establish the family unity – not simply because his overbearing behaviour has contributed powerfully to the disruption of relationships – but also because he is the father, and it is fitting that he should take paternal responsibility for his offspring. However, it would neither be appropriate nor convincing, if Rafe suddenly became a grovelling, apologetic figure: we would feel cheated. Despite his follies, in Rafe, Bill Naughton has created a character who merits respect: it would be unsatisfactory to diminish him in the interests of a facile happy ending.

Fortunately, as we have seen, Rafe is capable of learning from his mistakes: he has realized through bitter experience that the old, authoritarian methods no longer work. The attempt to impose his views upon 'children', who are rightly demanding that they should be allowed to make their own choices, has led to near-disaster. If Rafe is to merit consideration as a father, he must win his children's allegiance; in other words, they must exercise their freedom, and choose to love him and listen to his opinions, rather than have control exercised upon them from on high.

Rafe's method of achieving the love and respect of his children is simple, but imaginative. First he grants freedom where it is necessary: Florence and Arthur receive his blessing upon their marriage; Hilda is not opposed in her desire to leave home – they are all ready for the outside world. Secondly, by confessing that he has had to sacrifice his own freedom (and that he often felt like 'getting away from it all') in the family interest, he encourages his children to see him as a person, and to understand the responsibilities that he undertook when he became their father – and which he did not shirk. Thirdly, his apparent intention to leave the home establishes his value: his children become anxious and realize that he cannot be allowed to leave. He is asked to stay, he would be missed; he still has a rôle.

It is clear that Harold and Wilfred still need a home, also Florence and Hilda need a father, although they are beginning to make their own way in the world. Daisy, of course, needs a husband.

It should not come as a surprise that the Cromptons are reunited at the end of the play. Bill Naughton has indicated throughout that there is 'any amount of love' in the family and the crises have strengthened this bond. Rafe had always cared about his children: Daisy had always striven to maintain the peace. The play has shown us how the Cromptons are able to adapt to the change of circumstances brought about by the children's transition to adulthood.

two keys Rafe's handing over of the keys to his desk symbolizes his trust in Daisy; her acceptance of them indicates an acceptance of true responsibility. It is to be a more 'adult' relationship in the future.

grope your way . . . possible Rafe has abandoned the old certainties.

RAFE exits Dramatically necessary, if he is 'to think of some stroke'.

Get married Comedies have a tradition of ending in marriage: a symbol of harmony and happiness.

special licence i.e. without the formality of calling the banns.

expense . . . rebate Typical Crompton concerns!

we've all planned to leave home They are unaware of Rafe's change of heart.

pop! . . . uncle's Euphemisms for putting something in pawn.

you never . . . borrow another ha'penny Daisy is no longer going to be exploited as a 'soft touch'.

a hairpin A reminder of the time when Daisy intended to 'rob' the cash-box. Such deceptions will no longer be needed in the Crompton family.

but your own home? Rafe now gives wholehearted support to the marriage, and he wants things done properly.

having the choice Daisy and Rafe acknowledge the realities of their own situation. Bringing up a family entails the sacrifice of choice.

I wasn't born married The children are being given an important insight: their father sacrificed his own freedom of choice, so that they might have freedom and security. Almost a theological point.

very irresponsible Ironical; in fact it is a responsible action. Hilda is uneasy. She imagines that some harm may befall her father. Suicide?

he might never come back Wilfred contemplates life without his father.

Lodgings! It . . . struck me! The realities of independence are being brought home to Harold and Wilfred. They are not yet ready to accept them.

pull together, like? A change of heart.

no choice A reiteration of the idea that bringing up a family has entailed sacrifice of choice. The children are being dissuaded from an attitude of mindless rebellion. They are being given insight into the reality of what bringing up a family means – and learning to see their parents as human beings.

all come to an end True, but it is also a beginning.

A home . . . isn't love Another important truth. Despite appearances to the contrary, as Arthur later points out, there has always been love in the Crompton family.

'Course there is (love) This is a realization that has been brought home to the children.

doubts of late It has taken the crisis in the family to reveal the certainty of the presence of love. Everybody has learned by living through this troubled period. The capacity to learn from mistakes and to forgive has preserved the essential oneness of the Cromptons.

catches on Realizes that he is accepting orders from his younger brother. It is a comic reminder of the change of circumstances in the household.

Dad . . .! An enigmatic moment. Obviously it suggests the reconciliation of father and daughter. Perhaps, too, it indicates that she has realized that Rafe has engineered this reconciliation of the family; i.e. that his threat to leave was never a reality, but a 'stroke' (device) by means of which the family was made to realize his value and accept his implicit authority.

Revision questions on Act II Scene 3

1 Is there any evidence that Rafe has changed his attitude during the opening sequence of this scene?

2 Why is it ironic that Rafe offers Daisy 'some extra money'?

3 Describe what you take to be Daisy's feelings as she hears Wilfred recommending that his father should wear his new overcoat to the concert.

4 What is the effect of Daisy's confession upon Rafe?

5 Why do you think that Bill Naughton has Rafe describe his childhood at such length?

6 What do you think Rafe means when he says that he will 'think of some stroke'?

7 Why is it important that parents should not humble themselves before their children? Give reasons for your answer.

8 Do you think that Rafe really intended to leave home?

9 Do you think that Hilda is mature enough to leave home? Contrast Hilda with Wilfred and Harold, who decide to stay.

10 How does the final reconciliation come about? Give a detailed answer, taking your evidence from the entire scene.

Bill Naughton's art in
Spring and Port Wine
Characters

Rafe Crompton

I try to do good by force, and force seems to blind a man.

Rafe Crompton dominates the play. At the outset, as we watch Daisy struggling to manage the household finances, we are tempted to agree with Betsy Jane: Rafe must be a tyrant, who deprives even his wife of her pride and independence. Our first meeting with Rafe does not entirely confirm our initial impression: he has a quiet dignity of manner, he loves music and poetry; and, although he is clearly a man of rigid principle who expects to be obeyed, nonetheless he inspires affection in his wife. His children, although they are rebellious (with the exception of Florence), are sufficiently overawed to keep covert their antagonism. It is, however, time for a change in Rafe's domain.

A stern patriarch, Rafe's principles are based on traditional values: he abhors debt and the affectations of modernity; he appreciates good manners and he is suspicious of alcohol. He sets great store by the truth and believes in the absolute rightness of his own opinions, which are often reinforced by recourse to proverbial wisdom. There is nothing intrinsically wrong with Rafe's conservative beliefs, but problems arise because he seeks to enforce them rigidly, and they have become divorced from love and sensitivity. The play charts Rafe's progress towards self-understanding.

Rafe believes that good food should not be wasted: he has lived through the Hunger Marches of the 'Thirties, and he takes offence when Hilda refuses to eat her herring. His mistake, however, is to treat Hilda as though she is still a child, and he is wrong to discipline her in a childish manner.

Rafe's rigidity stands in the way of a humane perception of his daughter's choosing to refuse food that she does not want. The matter soon becomes inflated into a clash of wills, and neither father nor daughter is inclined to back down. Rafe lacks a sense of proportion. He is prepared to allow Hilda not to eat the herring, provided that she acknowledges his supremacy: by making a token gesture of eating it, she will have capitulated and his pride will be satisfied. Unfortunately, Hilda has inherited some of her father's pride, and her natural desire for independence is involved. No easy compromises are available.

Soon Rafe's pride and principles become even more deeply questioned, when Wilfred attempts to break the impasse by giving the herring to the cat. If there is one thing of which Rafe is certain, it is that truth is better than falsehood – and he proceeds to conduct an inquisition, which leads to Wilfred's breakdown. Once again, Rafe's rigid adherence to principle has prevented him from entering into an understanding that Wilfred's actions spring from a desire to preserve family harmony, and to help his sister. In short, Rafe is narrow-minded and intolerant. He also stands opposed to Florence's marriage – in this case, possibly from motives of jealousy of Aspinall's success, but whatever the reason, it is a choice which Florence herself should be allowed to make.

It is apparent that Rafe's essential interest is to maintain control over his family; over the years care has become confused with control. Although his morality is fundamentally sound, it is essentially Old Testament in character and lacks charity. As a consequence, he has stifled the freedom of his wife and family; he has become a stern god – to be appeased by grudging acquiescence and petty deceptions. So long as this state of affairs is maintained, Rafe is secure, but family life has become an embattled affair. It is a time for new insights.

Threatened with the dissolution of her family, Daisy defies her husband by breaking into the 'holy of holies' – the desk. By this time Rafe himself has become aware that the old ways must change. Significantly, in Act III, Scene 3, he apologizes to Wilfred for 'biting his head off', and asks Daisy's forgiveness for trying to 'do good by force'. At the same time Bill Naughton enhances our understanding of Rafe by having him relate his story of an unhappy debt-ridden childhood. It is clear that Rafe has the capacity to learn from his mistakes.

If, however, anything is to be salvaged from the wreckage of the Crompton family, then Rafe must be prepared not merely to recognize the error of his ways, but also to put into practice a new philosophy. It is too late to prevent Hilda from leaving home, and Florence will marry Arthur; Rafe has shown us that he is not happy with either of their decisions, but he recognizes his powerlessness in the circumstances, which he has helped to bring about. Deprived of the power to enforce his will, he is left only with the love of a father towards his children; and he now realizes that his children must be enabled to express the love which they possibly still feel towards him. Fortunately, there are reserves of love within the Crompton family upon which he can draw.

Rafe brings to the fore the love which has been latent in his family by giving away his power. Symbolically, he hands over the keys of his desk and cash-box; thus he begins by establishing a new, positive relationship with his wife: no longer will she need to practise deception upon him; a weight will be lifted from her shoulders, although she will now have to bear the responsibility of managing the money herself. However, she has been given pride and independence.

Rafe's willingness to accommodate his family's wishes startles them: faced with the realities of what leaving home means, they all come to recognize the value of the security which Rafe has provided. When he further reveals how he has sacrificed his own freedom for the sake of his family, then they realize that love has been present in the home, despite recent appearances to the contrary. Their need for him is sealed by his apparent decision to leave the house: they cannot bear to see him go.

Rafe has not ultimately sacrificed his position as head of the Cromptons. Circumstances have forced him to recognize that it is preferable to earn the love of his family, rather than seek to enforce his will. Daisy, Rafe and the children in the end agree to 'pull together' – and thus preserve family unity, even if some members of the family must leave for new pastures.

There is calculation in Rafe's magnanimity at the end of the play: his apparent, but unfulfilled, intention of leaving the house is a means by which he brings his children to recognize his value. It is a major insight. Adherence to routines and observances, whilst they may suffice for young children, have inevitably insufficient power to cement a family together indefinitely – children must be allowed to grow up and develop their own attitudes.

Rafe has been subtly characterized: we are constantly shifting our estimation of him. If the opening pages lead us to anticipate a tyrant, then we are forced to change our estimation as the play proceeds: his persecution of Hilda and Wilfred may be brutal, but there is a stature about the man as he demands *his* standards of his family, amidst the trivialities of the 'modern' world. There is great attraction in the certainties of the North-Country, Non-Conformist ethic. Rafe is also humanized by his love of the finer things of life: music and poetry in particular. His care for his family is self-evident, even if it is imposed upon them. Rafe has difficulty in adjusting to the needs of his 'adult' children: they inhabit a different world; he was brought up in the hard school of life. It is to his credit, however, that without sacrificing his dignity, he is able to adapt, and retrieve a potentially disastrous family situation.

Rafe, in common with the other members of his family, is set free. The events of the play have contrived to liberate him from the dominance of his unhappy childhood – which had led him to impose restraints upon his family, in an endeavour to save them from the misery of his early years.

Daisy
It shouldn't be a battle, Dad – bringing up a family.

Daisy's life has become a balancing act: not only must she literally balance the family budget (a task hampered by her innate generosity), but also she has to act as an intermediary between Rafe and his children. In promoting the welfare of her family, she has had to put her own needs in second place, and she has become adept at finding ways of pouring cups of tea on troubled waters.

Nonetheless, Daisy is disconcerted by Betsy Jane's remark that she lacks pride and independence. For the laudable motives of preserving peace and harmony, Daisy has sacrificed herself unremittingly – she has not lost her dignity, but she has become exploited. When Hilda refuses her herring, Daisy's instinctive reaction is to calm the situation and seek compromise. Unfortunately, neither Rafe nor Hilda is prepared to give way; as a consequence, Daisy is going 'humpbacked with worry' because of the conflict of loyalties which she is experiencing. Daisy's anxieties are increased when Arthur proposes to Florence. Daisy perceives that it is in her daughter's interests that the marriage should take place, but this brings her into conflict with her husband, who is deeply prejudiced against the match.

Tension mounts between Hilda and Rafe; again, Daisy tries to make Rafe see sense, but he remains unmoved – bringing up a family is indeed a battle. Caught in the crossfire, Daisy suffers as much, if not more, than the antagonists.

Daisy is a loyal and loving wife; she respects Rafe and his views, despite the fact that acting as a buffer between him and the children has become a burden to her – but soon she is forced to take sides. Rafe's inquisition of Wilfred and Hilda's determination to leave home brings to the fore her maternal instincts. She is horrified that her 'little boy' has been interrogated to breaking-point, and she cannot countenance the fact that Hilda ('always her father's favourite') has been driven to contemplate a hasty departure to London. Compromises are no longer available to Daisy. When she decides to break into Rafe's cash-box, she is appalled by her own actions – so much so, that she retreats from completing the task. Nonetheless, she asks Betsy Jane to pawn Rafe's overcoat, in the hope that she will be able to redeem it before he notices that it is missing. This is a last attempt at compromise. By chance, Rafe decides that he wants to wear the coat, leaving Daisy no recourse but to confront him with the bald fact that she has pawned it. She next launches upon a confession which culminates in a frank opinion of their relationship: she admits that she has deceived him over the family budgeting and that Rafe's standards are 'too much for me'.

Moved by what he has just heard, Rafe acknowledges that his wife possesses 'innate goodness', and he asks to be forgiven for his faults. In openly declaring the truth about what she feels, and thus eschewing her former belief that a mother should keep things to herself, Daisy initiates a new basis for the relationships within the family. Rafe now feels able to reveal his own feelings for her, and changes his attitude to Hilda. He is also prepared to give his blessing to the marriage of Florence and Arthur.

In this spirit of honesty and reconciliation, the family can be reunited. Ironically, when Rafe says that he intends to leave home, Daisy finds herself defending him; her role as an intermediary is not yet over, but on this occasion, her children do not need much persuading to support their father.

As they face their future, Daisy and Rafe can put the recent past into a comfortable perspective ('Happen we're a funny lot.'); it is as a result of these events that they can be free from the obstacles which had threatened to impede their relationship. The burden of fear has been lifted from Daisy's shoulders, and henceforth she can be more herself. In liberating herself (discovering pride and independence), Daisy has also inspired Rafe to acknowledge an important truth about himself: 'I try to do good by force . . . But the good you do, you do naturally, as though God were with you.' Daisy's charitable spirit has come to permeate the play.

Hilda

Her father's favourite – and look what he's driven her to.

Hilda, nineteen years old, is presented as a girl who has been influenced by the trappings of 'modernity': she reads *Weekend* magazine, she dresses 'fashionably', and she partakes of port wine, which seems to have a liberating effect upon her! Also, she has a failed love-affair behind her. She is not a trivial girl, however, and her defiance of her father suggests that she has an uncompromising nature. She also has the courage to stand her ground despite the pressure which is exerted upon her to give in. Furthermore, Hilda actually decides that it is time for her to leave the home – even if she does not quite manage to go to London, she nonetheless makes arrangements to go and live with her friend, Betty Partington.

Hilda's refusal of the herring, trivial in itself, precipitates the crisis in the family. Her plan to eat it all, in order to discomfort Rafe, shows a shrewd understanding of his character: it reveals that she perceives that her father has sufficient sympathy with her to feel upset by such an action. In other words, she understands that he is not a heartless tyrant, and that he would not require her to eat the herring in its entirety. It should not surprise us that she has this understanding of her father; despite their conflict, it is evident that she shares many of Rafe's characteristics. She also has Daisy's sensitivity: she apologizes for the trouble which she has caused her mother, and their conversations reveal their mutual rapport.

Hilda's decision to leave for London shows her to be impulsive and there is a vulnerability about her which is emphasized by the occasional suggestion that she may be pregnant. However, she is also realistic: Betty Partington's house is a more sensible haven than 'The Smoke'. She has the honesty to admit that she is a 'softie' and she is discriminating enough to express typical Crompton distaste for Betsy Jane's 'muckiness'.

Hilda is an attractive character, who carries with her the freshness and vitality of youth. In terms of maturity, she is probably the most ready of all the Crompton offspring to leave home. Furthermore, the spring-like freshness of Hilda's character melts the wintry attitudes and routines of the Crompton family. Her refusal to eat the herring triggers a change in the relationship between Daisy and Rafe; and Arthur's gesture of sympathy towards her in her plight inspires jealousy in her sister, which, in turn, leads the static engagement of Arthur and Florence to blossom into marriage.

Florence

I don't believe in rushing things.

At the outset, Florence enjoys a comfortable existence: she is a schoolteacher and may therefore be presumed to have moved from the working class to the middle class. But her working-class roots are secure: she is devoted to her father and supports him absolutely – attending to his needs and echoing his ideas. She is also comfortable with her mother, who is grateful for her arithmetical help. She has the security of a long-standing engagement to Arthur. In common with the other characters in the play, she experiences some shocks, which shake her complacency.

Arthur's proposal that he and Florence get married 'soon like', forces Florence to face an issue which had remained happily dormant: marriage means leaving the reassuring nest, and also, as it turns out, defying the wishes of her father. In essence, Florence is being asked to make a mature emotional commitment to Arthur, and along with it go all the responsibilities of making a home. Florence has only known one home, and her emotional needs have been focused on her father, whom she clearly worships. Will Florence have the courage to leave home and establish herself elsewhere?

At first, Florence instinctively withdraws from the prospects which have been offered her – she refuses to be rushed. Ironically, it is jealousy of Hilda which provokes the apparently cold schoolmistress to throw herself passionately into Arthur's arms: fearing that she may lose him, she responds to his declaration that he loves her.

Circumstances contrive to liberate Florence: she comes into the house 'bursting' with the news that she is going to get married. By this time, Rafe himself has changed his outlook and she receives her father's full support.

Harold

After all, we are living in a democracy, you know.

Harold is a lively young man, full of jokes and smart asides. He enjoys teasing Wilfred and his sisters, and smokes and gambles in defiance of his father's wishes – but he is careful to keep such activities hidden – as we see when he frantically tries to rid the room of cigarette smoke on the approach of his father. Harold has plenty of bravado, but essentially he is a conformist; he may go so far as to be insolent to Rafe, but he joins in the family singing (albeit reluctantly), whilst it is Wilfred who actually rebels and takes the pressure off Hilda.

During the play, Harold becomes more serious-minded and mature: he senses that the 'inquest' over the herring has gone 'far enough' and registers a protest early in the proceedings. His developing sensitivity is further demonstrated when he perceives his father to be 'a man lost', and he tactfully suggests that it would be better if Rafe was not present when the girls return to collect their things, prior to their departure. Also, it is Harold who decides to 'put the block' on Rafe's apparent determination to leave the house.

Harold resolves not to leave the house at the end of the play. Like Wilfred, he is not quite ready to quit the security of home. Thus it is relevant that Harold proposes that the family should hang on and 'give it another go' and 'pull together, like'. These remarks come from the heart, and incidentally give Rafe a further reason for not departing: he still has the vestiges of a family to father. It is a measure of the change wrought in Rafe that the most vociferous of the rebels should plead for him to stay.

Wilfred

I felt I couldn't bear to see it put in front of our Hilda again.

Wilfred is the 'baby' of the family. He is loving towards his mother and shows her particular sympathy in times of stress. His affectionate nature is further revealed by his vain attempt to save Hilda from having to eat the herring. Unfortunately, his plan misfires and he has to endure a harrowing interrogation. This is an important moment in the play: Rafe is revealed as a bully in attacking the most

vulnerable and well-meaning of his children; as a consequence Daisy's maternal instincts are sufficiently aroused for
her to confront Rafe with the enormity of what he has done.
The incident also precipitates Hilda's departure and
Arthur's telling remark that Rafe has used the Bible 'for his
own purposes'. Finally, the episode underlines Rafe's insensitivity in not appreciating the basically humane motives
which prompted Wilfred's deception.

It is not surprising that Wilfred's intention of leaving
home evaporates so easily: of all the members of the Crompton family he is probably the least ready to strike out on his
own. For much of the play, he has to play second fiddle to
Harold's more articulate rebelliousness, and he is often the
butt of brotherly teasing. But Wilfred's instincts are all
sound: he is a true son of his mother – a person who does good
'naturally' and puts his own needs last. At the end of the
play, he is happy to accept philosophically the traumas
which have rocked the family: 'I suppose we could go further
and fare worse.'

Arthur

. . . there's any amount of love in this house! Even I can see that.

Arthur's talents have given him the chance of improving his
lot, but his proposal to Florence that they get married
immediately brings him into conflict with Rafe, and he
consequently finds himself deeply embroiled in the family
problems. Although he is not yet married to Florence, he is
already, in a sense, part of the family, but he could, if he
wished, withdraw and not marry Florence. It is a measure,
therefore, of his resolve and courage that he pursues his love
for her, in spite of the formidable obstacles. He does not
cower in front of Rafe; although he admits he is 'mithered' by
the case against marriage, he nonetheless doggedly puts his
point of view. When Rafe interrogates Wilfred, Arthur

boldly states his opinion and rebukes him for using the Bible for his own purposes. Arthur is sympathetic to Hilda in her moment of distress, which eventually leads Florence to agree to an 'early' marriage. Thus, we find Arthur a wholly likable character who voices opinions with which we can identify. His remark that there is 'any amount of love in this house', shows him to be perceptive and it sets the seal on the rediscovered harmony in the Crompton family.

Because he comes from outside the family, Arthur brings important insights, and, as we have seen, he has the courage to state them at crucial moments in the play. Rafe may not enjoy Arthur's blunt declarations, but he respects his willingness to state his mind. In confronting his prospective father-in-law with home truths, Arthur makes an important contribution to the development of the family's relationships.

Betsy Jane

Good hearted – ee, but I couldn't live there. (Hilda)

Betsy Jane, like Daisy, is constantly in debt; she is an inefficient housekeeper and has no compunction about deceiving her husband. Ironically, she accuses Daisy of having no 'pride and independence', whilst apparently unaware that she is similarly deficient. This does not deny the validity of Betsy Jane's insight, which sets Daisy thinking seriously about her relationship with Rafe; but, unlike Daisy, Betsy Jane will never change – despite her husband's big win on the horses, she remains in debt.

For all her dubious ways, however, Betsy Jane remains a likable character – her good-heartedness is evident in her lack of hesitation in giving succour to Hilda – and she is only too willing to lend Daisy her skills as a picker of locks.

As well as making an important contribution to the plot of the play, Betsy Jane has a useful role as Daisy's confidante.

Her appearances, whilst often of thematic relevance, also contribute to a relaxation of tension after moments of high drama in the Crompton household.

Themes

The family

Bill Naughton presents us with a drama of family life. The Cromptons are put under the microscope and we observe how they deal with their crisis of relationships. The setting is familiar and precise: the Cromptons are a working-class family; they live in Bolton, Lancashire, during the early-to-mid 1960s. Inevitably, we are reminded of *Coronation Street* – the evergreen television 'soap-opera'. The characters are all recognizable as 'types'. Thus Rafe is the overbearing father, who has old-fashioned views; Daisy is the good-hearted, much put-upon mother; Hilda is the young woman, who, influenced by 'modern' notions, seeks to assert her own personality in what has become a restrictive environment. The other characters may similarly be identified as 'types' – which is not to deny that Bill Naughton has also successfully individualized them. The situations in the play are familiar, too: there is an abiding worry of the Cromptons about money; concern over the refusal of 'good food'; there is a 'clash of the generations'. To suggest that the characters and situations in the play are familiar, should not be taken as adverse criticism: Bill Naughton clearly wants his play to be accessible, and familiarity helps us to identify with the characters and their predicaments. *Spring and Port Wine*, however, is more than just 'a slice of life' play, which rehashes well-worn conflicts of family relationships. The ingredients may be stereotypical, but Bill Naughton's organization of his material is sensitive; his themes are universal, and subtly analysed.

Leaving Home

At some stage in the play all the Cromptons contemplate the prospect of leaving home. Of course, it is part of the normal development of a family that, sooner or later, children should develop sufficient independence to enable them to depart from the family environment in order to fashion their own lives. Such a process implies change: parents have to understand that they cannot expect to govern the lives of their children indefinitely; and children have to come to understand their parents in a new light – so that their departure is not destructive of harmonious human relationships. It is probably true to say that some pain cannot be avoided during this natural process; it would not be human if parents did not experience some area of sadness at the departure of a much-loved son or daughter. Similarly, even the most independent offspring may well feel some trepidation as they face the prospect of life without the reassurance of the immediate presence of mother and father. Nonetheless, it is to be hoped that most families can come to terms with these 'facts of life', without undue trauma.

Spring and Port Wine, however, dramatizes this basic human situation in such a way that the Cromptons very nearly do come to grief. The problems centre on Rafe, who is highly-principled, but dictatorial. As we have seen, it is his belief that he has the absolute right (invested in him by his position as the father of the Crompton family) to determine the moral and social behaviour of his wife and family. It is inevitable that he comes into conflict with his children. Rafe is portrayed as being old-fashioned in his views: it offends him that his children smoke, read trashy material and do not appear to share his tastes in music and poetry with appropriate enthusiasm. This should not be taken to mean that he is wrong; indeed, Rafe's love of quality in all its aspects is presented by Bill Naughton as one of his most endearing characteristics. But problems arise simply because his children inhabit a different world, where mass culture is highly influential. In this world, it is not regarded as suspicious to read *Weekend* and *News of the World*; nor is it morally dubious to consume alcohol in moderation. These and other such differences of cultural/social behaviour, in themselves, are relatively trivial: most families have the resilience to come to terms with such disparities of viewpoint. Rafe, however, cannot encompass any deviation from the patterns of behaviour which he has established without believing that the whole edifice of family-life will come crashing down. It is not surprising, therefore, that as his children approach adulthood, so the atmosphere of crisis deepens.

It may be helpful if we focus upon the central point of contention in the play: Hilda's herring. At first sight, it seems absurd that such an incident should become so magnified that it threatens the entire family, but there is an element of truth in Florence's accusation – '. . . you caused it all- . . . Why didn't you eat that bloody herring' (page 71).

It is convincing that such a trivial matter has such dire repercussions: family quarrels often have humble origins. Also, it is probably not coincidental that Bill Naughton chose Hilda's refusal to eat 'good food' to be the point of contention: in demanding that Hilda eat the herring, Rafe is reiterating the age-old requirement that children should consume what is put before them – in other words he is treating her as a child. Thus, in her refusal to comply, Hilda is implicitly refusing to be so treated – she is demanding to be given adult status and freedom of choice. The incident also relates to Rafe's experience of the past (the Hunger Marchers) and emphasizes the generation gap – Hilda lives in an age of comparative plenty.

The scope of the conflict is widened, as the Crompton family takes sides. Only Florence unequivocally supports her father; she perceives that the herring is a 'matter of

principle'. It is soon apparent that Hilda's defiance of her
father has exposed latent tensions in the family: such has
been the dominance of Rafe that for many years the Cromptons have been forced to evade contentious issues, rather
than face them openly. Obviously, some of these tensions are
peculiar to the Crompton family, but many of them are
inherent in all families. Strategies have evolved in this game
of psychological warfare. Therefore, things have become
rather complicated. Daisy, for example, has long en-
deavoured to manage the financial accounts by borrowing
and cooking the books; Rafe has been aware of these deceptions, but has been content to go along with them. When
Hilda wishes to discomfort her father, she says that she
intends to eat all of the herring – thus denying Rafe the
satisfaction of magnanimously giving in to her, if she will
only make an attempt to eat it.

Hilda's stubbornness stimulates her brothers to defiance,
and when it is coupled with Florence's marriage to Arthur
and Daisy's breaking into the desk – and the apparent
determination of them all to leave home – it is not surprising
that Rafe senses that he must change, if his family is to
remain together. His authority has broken down.

'I can smell rebellion in the air . . .'

Rafe's family love and respect him, but they also fear him. If
he is defied, then Rafe is prone to bully his family into
submission. Sometimes his wrath can be terrifying, as we see
when Wilfred is subjected to a relentless inquisition. Rafe is
prepared to starve Hilda into acquiescence. True, Rafe
probably knows that Daisy will come to the aid of those who
suffer at his hands – but there must be better ways of
persuading his children of the rightness of his principles. In
any event, Daisy is constantly put in the difficult position of
having to act as the buffer between Rafe's sometimes un-

reasonable demands and the wishes of the children. Inevitably, she suffers. And we are forced to conclude that imposing his will is more important to Rafe than the unhappiness he causes.

Young children are inclined to accept unquestioningly the authority of their father, but in this play Bill Naughton examines that moment in a child's development when authority is questioned: Hilda (and to some extent the other children) are on the threshold of adulthood – and the old dictatorial methods no longer work. *Spring and Port Wine* examines and dramatizes this age-old 'problem' of authority in the context of family relationships. We may note, in passing, a parallel with Shakespeare's *King Lear*.

The consequences of the breakdown of Rafe's authority, based as it is upon fear, are vividly demonstrated. The Cromptons, as a family unit, lose their bearings. Father is set against child and wife against husband. If they are to be saved from total dissolution, the Cromptons must learn to '. . . pull together, like . . .'

We have concentrated so far upon the forces which disrupt the Cromptons: in particular, the clash of generations; Rafe's intransigence and bullying; Hilda's obstinacy; the natural desire of children to break free from the family and develop their independence; the petty deceits and lack of frankness which have become a necessary means of avoiding conflict. But the final note of the play is reconciliation; the Cromptons surmount these problems, undergo change and are, in a sense, reborn.

Despite the tensions which erupt into outright discord, there have always been forces which bind the family together. On a simple level, underneath the disharmony, the Cromptons clearly have much in common. For all his faults, Rafe is portrayed as fundamentally a decent man; he may be misguided but the play shows that he is capable of learning from his mistakes. Ironically, the discord is a means whereby he comes to learn the error of his ways. It is not an easy process and we watch him undergoing the pain of a man 'lost' – as he comes to appreciate the suffering that he has inflicted upon his wife and children. Gradually, however, he comes to understand that an *imposed* authority is no longer viable, and he gives Hilda, Daisy and Florence their freedom. This independence, does not, however, lead to the disruption of the family-unit – paradoxically, in granting them their liberty, he binds the family closer together and discovers a new sort of authority. This authority is based upon love, not fear; it is freely given, not imposed. Once fear has been driven out, then the love which has always been present in the family (manifest in their underlying care for one another) comes to the surface.

If there are natural forces which tend to cause division in the family, equally there are forces which unite them. Thus, Daisy and Rafe must remain together because there is nowhere else for them to go: they made their vows in St Philip's Church and accepted the responsibilities of marriage – it is inconceivable that they should part; they have shared their lives; they have brought up their family. Wilfred and Harold, for all their apparent determination to leave home, are not yet quite mature enough to undertake such a step; their turn will come – and will doubtless be achieved without the trauma which afflicted Hilda and Florence.

If Rafe has learned some important lessons during the play, so have his offspring. Over the years, as a response to the insensitive treatment they had received, the children had come to take Rafe for granted; to some extent they had ceased to regard him as a person, and looked upon him as a tyrant to be appeased. So resentful have they become, that they begrudge him a new overcoat. But, as they contemplate his loss, so they come to rediscover his value. Thus the reconciliation of the family is a two-way process. It is part of Rafe's new insight into the way relationships can be made to flourish, that he has the imagination to facilitate this process, by facing his children with the prospect of his departure.

Discord in the play is seen to be an educative force, and because the play is a comedy, the characters are 'permitted' to enjoy the fruits of their discoveries about themselves and each other. Nonetheless, the pain which the discord produces, while it lasts, is acute – and no one suffers more than Daisy. Daisy has the capacity to identify with all the other characters in the play, and consequently she endures most, as she watches her family seeming to fall apart. However, her innate generosity of spirit points the way forward for the Cromptons. She obviously inspires love in her children, and it is a key moment of self-realization for Rafe when he perceives the suffering which he has inflicted upon his wife: 'Nay you must forgive me . . . I try to do good by force, and force seems to blind a man. But the good you do you do naturally, as though God were there with you.'

Conclusion

Whilst it is not overtly a religious play, it is impossible to escape the Christian overtones which pervade the drama. We have already noticed in the character studies that Rafe is presented as a man imbued with a Non-Conformist faith. There are echoes of the Genesis story in Hilda's refusal to eat the herring, which remind us of Eve's eating of the apple. In both cases, freedom and obedience to authority are made to centre upon an apparently trivial matter of eating (or not eating) a humble item of food. The notion of giving away authority in order to maintain authority has parallels in the Christian paradox of God whose divinity comprises humility and whose service is perfect freedom. Above all, the play seems to exemplify the Christian virtue of Charity – as a force for healing and reconciliation.

Setting

The play is set in a working-class home, located in Bolton, Lancashire. References to the cotton-mill where Rafe, Hilda, Wilfred and Harold all work remind us that the wealth of the city was founded upon cotton, although nowadays the industry has declined – and the Lancashire cotton-mill is a comparative rarity. One of the reasons for the particularly close-knit quality of family life may be attributed to the fact that most working men and women shared employment in the same industry. In common with many of their contemporaries, the Cromptons' entertainment derives from a common interest in football (Bolton Wanderers) and classical music – especially choral works. Music often provided a ready escape from the tedium and hardship of industrial life.

Spring and Port Wine depicts the Cromptons during a time of transition, and change is evident in the wider context of North-Country traditions. We can detect the influence of mass communications upon Hilda, who reads a mass circulation magazine and is lured by the promise offered by 'emigrating' to London. Even Wilfred reads the *News of the World* and Daisy listens to *Housewives' Choice*. One of the attractions of the new home offered to Arthur is that it will possess a telephone. A television is a feature of the Crompton living room.

The Cromptons' house, with its living room, kitchen and scullery is typical of working-class homes in the North. The living room reflects the expectations and attitudes of Rafe and Daisy: it is cared-for and orderly – it contains nothing tawdry, reflecting a love of quality; but it is no match for the house which Florence and Arthur will inhabit, with its gable-end and new bath. Florence and Arthur are clearly destined for the middle class and a caravan near the coast!

From the affectionate way he delineates the Cromptons and their home, we may guess that Bill Naughton feels much affection for the 'old-fashioned' ways which were part of his own early experiences. The new world, for all its attractions, seems to be depicted as inferior and lacking in warmth. But Bill Naughton is realistic: he recognizes that change is inevitable and he does not over-emphasize the inferiority of the new. It is an important contribution to the overall optimistic tone of the play that all the characters are shown to be capable of learning about themselves and the changing circumstances in which they live. They do not abandon the essential virtues of the old ways – indeed, new virtues are acquired – so that they are able to adjust to change, without being destroyed by it.

Style

Spring and Port Wine is a naturalistic play: it creates the illusion that we are watching 'real' characters, living their lives against a realistic background. The dialogue gives the Cromptons substance as they express their thoughts, feelings and interests; it defines the changes in their relationships and gives us information about their past, present and expectations for the future. Bill Naughton writes dialogue for his characters which is appropriate to the North-Country setting of the play: it is lucid but unmistakeably Lancastrian in vocabulary and turns of phrase. Words such as 'codding', 'summat' and 'gradely', and expressions such as 'bide you there' are indicative of the characters' background – and, whilst some may require 'translation' for southern audiences, they are not obtrusive. But they remind us of the play's locale; also, because all the characters share these speech mannerisms, they serve to remind us that there are bonds of common culture which unite them, despite their differences. In this context, we may note that the characters tend to call each other 'love', and speak of 'our' Florence; Rafe calls Daisy 'mother'. Again, these are North-Country speech mannerisms – although not exclusively so.

It is a measure of Bill Naughton's skill as a dramatist that he is able to differentiate his characters by means of the dialogue. For example, Rafe is much given to short sentences and aphorism; in this way something of his dogmatic nature is revealed. He also has a reflective tone, which is often manifest in his long speeches when he describes his past. On these occasions, his words rise to a level of 'poetic' prose, as he recalls the vivid emotions which he once felt. His memories, however, are usually focused on specific incidents, which are pithily described in stark language ('I came home from school one dinner-time . . . to gas herself at the gas stove'). In contrast, Daisy's tone is altogether softer: she does not hector, her words tend to be more positive; she is less inclined to speak negatively; she is, however, prepared to speak her mind, and her pronouncements, when they come, carry weight; her concern is more for the individual; she has a more comforting manner than her husband. She is sometimes flustered, however, and on such occasions her speech becomes staccato. When Rafe is about to go and fetch his overcoat, she raises her voice – a rarity – which is indicative of the panic she feels.

The Crompton children share the same basic characteristics as their parents in terms of their speech-modes. Wilfred has his mother's softness, but Hilda, like her father, has moments of dogmatism, yet shares her mother's tone of gentle concern. Harold is the wit of the family and his sotto voce barbs sometimes act as an ironic commentary on the words and actions of his father. The children, in general, adopt a more modern idiom, which reveals the influence of the contemporary world and sometimes reflects their 'distance' from their father.

In accordance with the North-Country tradition of directness, all the Cromptons (and Arthur) 'speak their minds' when the occasion demands, and their imagery, frequently drawn from everyday experience, is often vivid ('It was like a nightmare over the home'). It seems that the Cromptons are a family for whom words still matter. They are all capable of producing a striking phrase in an unaffected manner.

The texture of the play is further enriched by the inclusion of poetry, music and song. Bill Naughton uses music to create atmosphere. Song, as well as being intrinsically enjoyable, stresses the common heritage of the family. Dialogue, poetry, music and song combine to give the play variety of expression. Rafe's experience of life and his self-education give him a greater range of reference than the other characters; his speech is the most vivid of the Cromptons – but all the characters to some extent are influenced by him, and consequently the play is imbued with his richness of expression. Bill Naughton's dialogue, in general, convincingly encompasses a great variety of moods – ranging from moments of quiet intimacy to those times when the family seems gripped by spasms of destructive quarrelling.

Stage Directions

Bill Naughton's stage directions often give detailed indications of how he wishes the play to be staged. The direction which opens the play reflects the tastes and interests of the Crompton family – Rafe, in particular. Sometimes the stage directions give brief pen portraits of the characters, even down to such details as handbags, for example. Furthermore, Bill Naughton often indicates how he wants the characters to be grouped on stage, so that their relationships can be made theatrically vivid to the audience. Sometimes a character's inner feelings are directly stated, at other times they are revealed by indication of a specific gesture or movement. These directions are not superfluous but show that Bill Naughton has a precise visualization of how he wants his play to appear to an audience. They are very helpful to the reader of the play because they enable us to bring setting, movement and character to life in our mind's eye.

A note on comedy

It is not hard to imagine that the problems which the Cromptons confront might have resulted in tragedy. There are moments in the play when we feel dissension predominates – yet Bill Naughton entitles his play 'A Comedy'. Of course, it is too crude a notion that comedy necessarily entails unremitting laughter, although there is much in the play which is self-evidently 'funny'. For example, Harold obviously contributes to the lightness of tone with his jokes; his teasing sense of humour sometimes releases the tension in fraught situations. Similarly, we find much direct humour in the character of Betsy Jane, whose amoral way of life contrasts with that of the virtuous Daisy.

We also find ironic humour in the play, when we see characters becoming involved in situations which they could not foresee and which they would least desire. At such times it may be a grim humour, but we never laugh *at* the characters; our amusement is always sympathetic.

However, despite the potential disasters which face the Cromptons, the play remains essentially a good-natured comedy. The outcome is happy: the characters change – they are not destroyed by the troubles which beset them – they learn from their mistakes and arrive at a better understanding of themselves and each other. Even the most threatening moments resolve themselves on a note of harmony: Hilda does not venture too far from the home; Rafe comes to the aid of the stricken Wilfred; Arthur and Florence are to be married, despite Rafe's initial misgivings. No character is malevolent and the play ends optimistically, with the resolve 'to pull together'. Throughout the play, Bill Naughton has kept before us the positive, loving side of his characters – the presiding movement of the play is towards reconciliation.

General questions on the play

1 'A home can be a prison where there isn't love.' Discuss the relevance of Rafe's comment with reference to the play as a whole.

Guideline notes for an answer

—— Rafe's remark at the end of the play is an important insight.

a) Rafe has denied freedom to his home, family, etc. – in this sense, the home has become a prison without bars.

—Daisy a prisoner to weekly accounts; Hilda must eat herring; Florence must not marry. Also more trivial rules about smoking, etc.

b) Despite restraints:

—Daisy loves Rafe; Rafe's values are often sound (if conservative and old-fashioned). Also, children and Daisy manifest mutual concern and love; discipline can be an aspect of caring.

c) The rules are challenged:

—by Harold, Wilfred; and more significantly by Hilda, who refuses to be treated like a child. N.B. Florence decides to marry Arthur against her father's wishes. Daisy breaks into Rafe's desk.

d) Can the family survive a change in the order of things? What will happen when the authoritarian restraints/régime, imposed by Rafe, break down?

e) Daisy's self-assertion *vis-à-vis* Rafe is crucial – manifest after Wilfred's breakdown and in her siding with Hilda.

—In siding with them, asserts her own independence.

—Symbolically casts off money shackles – breaks into desk.

f) Apparent impasse: the rules are no longer in force. The walls of the 'prison' have been breached. The old authority no longer holds sway. Can the Cromptons survive as a family?

g) Rafe asks forgiveness. Admits he was wrong to make his family fear him. Daisy and Rafe reaffirm their love. The family will remain together because they all recognize the bonds of love which unite them.

h) Presence of love already established (see b):

—But fear threatened to drive out love.

—Love reawakened by living through the crisis, and by Rafe's managing to re-establish his worth as a father to his children (N.B. the threat of his absence).

i) Once love re-established: freedom can follow, without dissolution of essential family bonds.

—Florence can marry Arthur; Hilda can leave, but not for the insecurities of London; Harold and Wilfred decide to stay. All will 'pull together'.

j) Conclusion:

The events of the play have presented the family in crisis, but a new order and fresh insights have emerged from the disruption.

—The children have come to appreciate Rafe (and Daisy) as persons, who because of their sacrifices have earned respect and love. Rafe, in particular, has come to be valued, rather than feared.

—Rafe has come to understand the natural needs of his children, who are now young adults, and therefore have the right to exercise choice. He has been liberated from his own past.

—Rafe and Daisy can re-establish their relationship, free from pretences and anxiety.

—All can be themselves, without needing to 'keep up a front'. They have all been, in a sense, set free from the old restraints.

2 Show how the character of Rafe is developed during the play.

3 Explain the significance of the play's title.

4 What does the play tell us about the nature of family conflicts?

5 Discuss the significance of the herring and the overcoat.

6 What importance do you attach to the role of Arthur?

7 Discuss the contribution of Betsy Jane to the play.

8 Discuss and illustrate the clash of values in the play.

9 What characteristics are shared by the Cromptons?

10 Do you find any ambiguities in Rafe's behaviour during the final scene:

11 Why do Harold and Wilfred decide not to leave home?

12 In what ways does Bill Naughton give his play a North-Country flavour?

13 Do you agree with Florence that Hilda 'caused it all'?

14 'Knots were made to be unfastened.' Discuss the thematic relevance of this remark.

15 How far do you think Rafe was a prisoner of his early environment?

16 'Without Daisy the play might have been a tragedy, rather than a comedy.' Estimate Daisy's contribution to the resolution of the conflict.

17 From your own experience, devise a case-study of a family which comes to terms with the 'clash of generations'.

18 How far do you think parents have the right to determine the behaviour and tastes of their children?

19 Imagine that the play had been set in a small country village in the south of England. How would the story of the Cromptons have been different?

20 Suppose that Hilda *had* departed for London after leaving the house. Tell her story.

Further Reading

Other works by Bill Naughton:

A Roof Over One's Head
Rafe Granite
One Small Boy
Alfie
Alfie Darling
Late Night on Watling Street
The Goal Keeper's Revenge
A Dog Called Nelson
My Pal Spadger
On the Pig's Back (autobiographical)